ABSURDITIES

MATERNAL INSTINCT

ABSURDITIES

W. HEATH ROBINSON

DUCKWORTH

Second Impression 1977

This edition first published in 1975 by
Gerald Duckworth & Co. Ltd.
The Old Piano Factory
43 Gloucester Crescent, London NW1.

ISBN 0 7156 0920 3

Absurdities was compiled by Heath Robinson himself at the height of his
fame and was the only large-scale general collection of his humorous work
published during his lifetime. When it first appeared in 1934, there was a
limited edition of 250 copies signed by the artist, in addition to two ordinary,
popular editions.

In this reissue nine of the *Absurdities* drawings which have already been
reprinted in *Inventions* (1973) are replaced with new material which has not
so far appeared in any of his books. The nine old drawings are 'How Noah
Averted a Catastrophe', 'Sale-time Improvements', 'Testing Scent
Discrimination in Young Foxhounds', 'Multi-Tennis', 'Clam Spearing in the
Frozen North', 'Testing Artificial Teeth in a Modern Tooth Works', 'A Surprise
Packet for the Cat Burglar', 'Modesty' and 'Kinematographing the Crocodile'.
These appear (some with slightly different titles) on pp. 64, 112, 45, 18, 38,
59, 136, 127 and 42 of *Inventions*. The nine new drawings for *Absurdities* are
those appearing here on pp. 11, 15, 18, 49, 53, 55, 69, 80 and 91.

Printed in Great Britain
by Unwin Brothers Limited
The Gresham Press, Old Woking, Surrey, England
A member of the Staples Printing Group

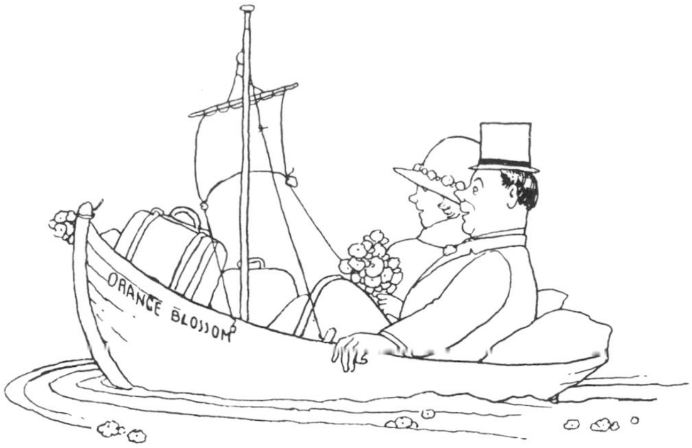
ORANGE BLOSSOM

WHITHER?

CONTENTS

CONTENTS

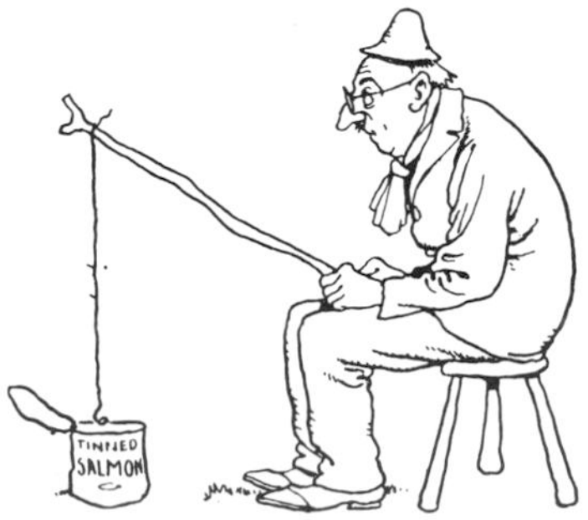
TINNED
SALMON

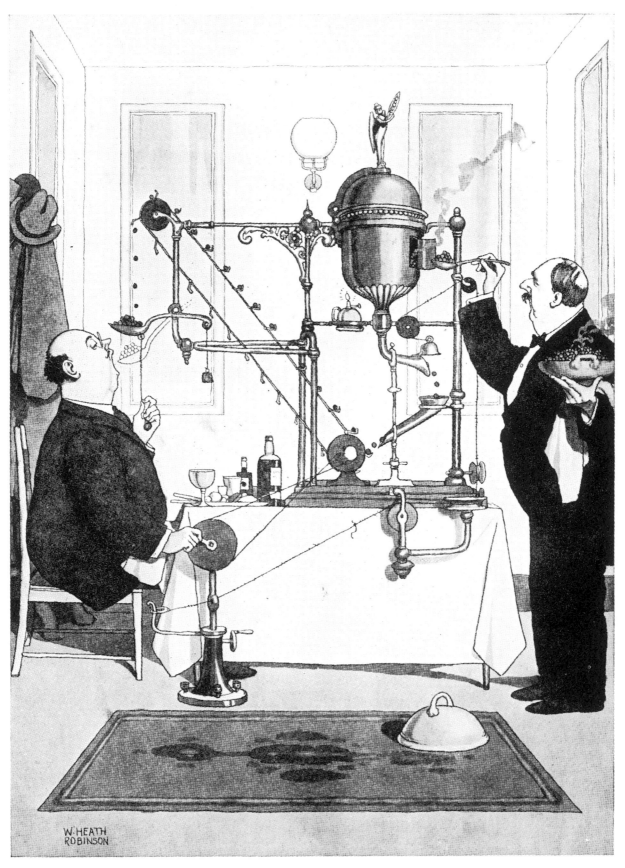

AN INTERESTING AND ELEGANT APPARATUS DESIGNED TO OVERCOME ONCE FOR
ALL THE DIFFICULTIES OF CONVEYING GREEN PEAS TO THE MOUTH

THE HOLE IN THE SPORRAN
A tale of accumulating interest

PLUCKY ATTEMPT TO RESCUE A FAMILY OVERTAKEN BY THE TIDE

HOW TO OBTAIN A GOOD NIGHT'S SLEEP IN SPITE OF INTERRUPTIONS

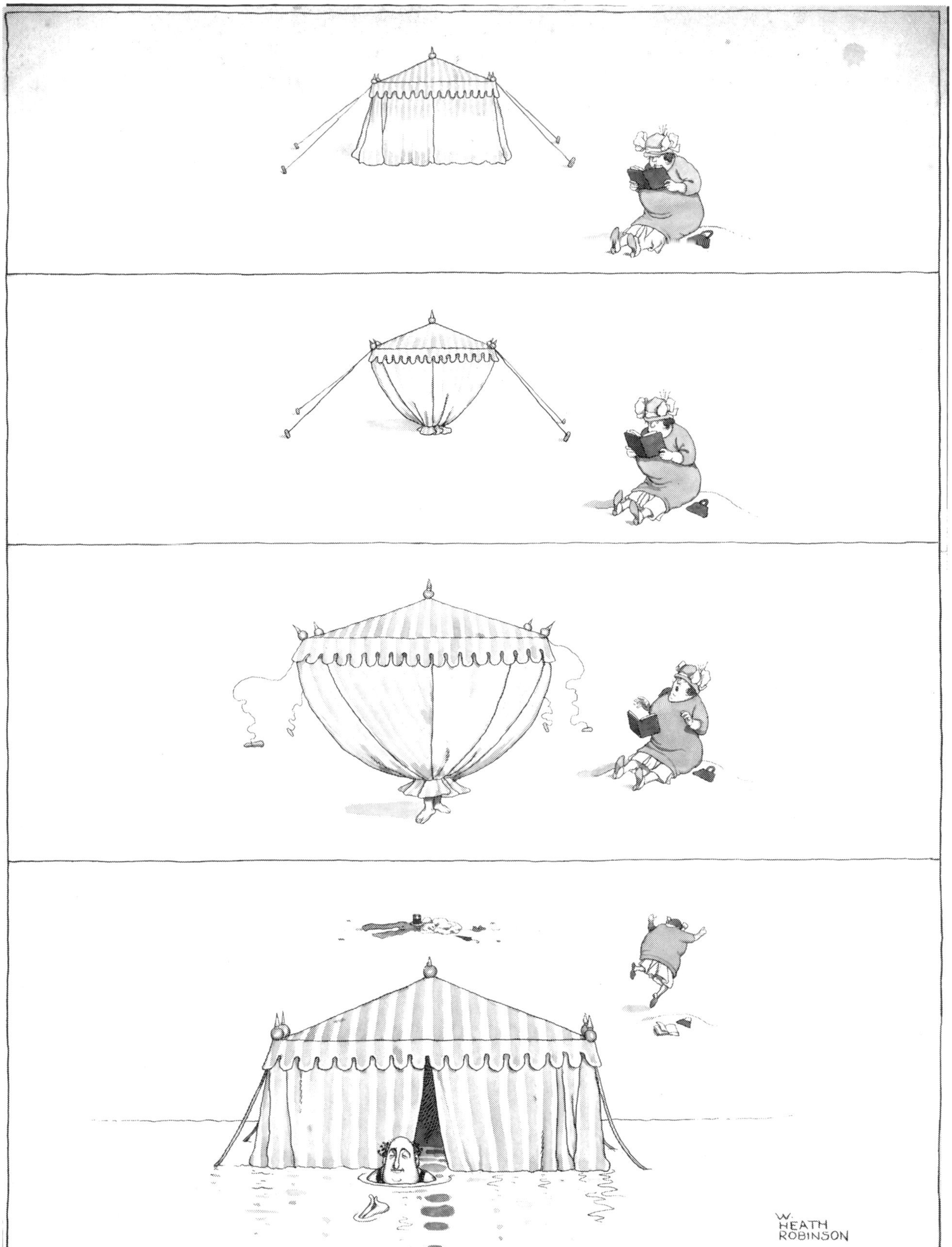
W. HEATH ROBINSON

MODESTY

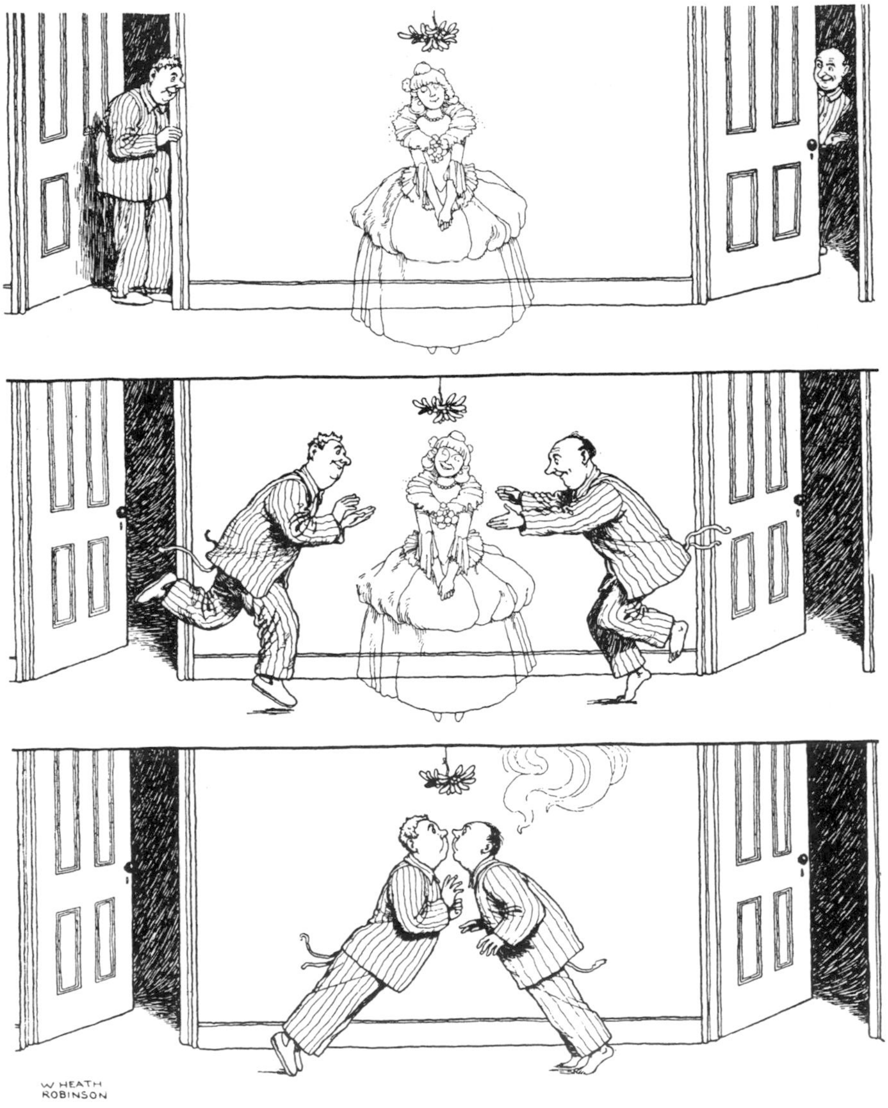
W. HEATH
ROBINSON

THE GHOST

TORTOISE COURSING
A pastime for the peacefully disposed

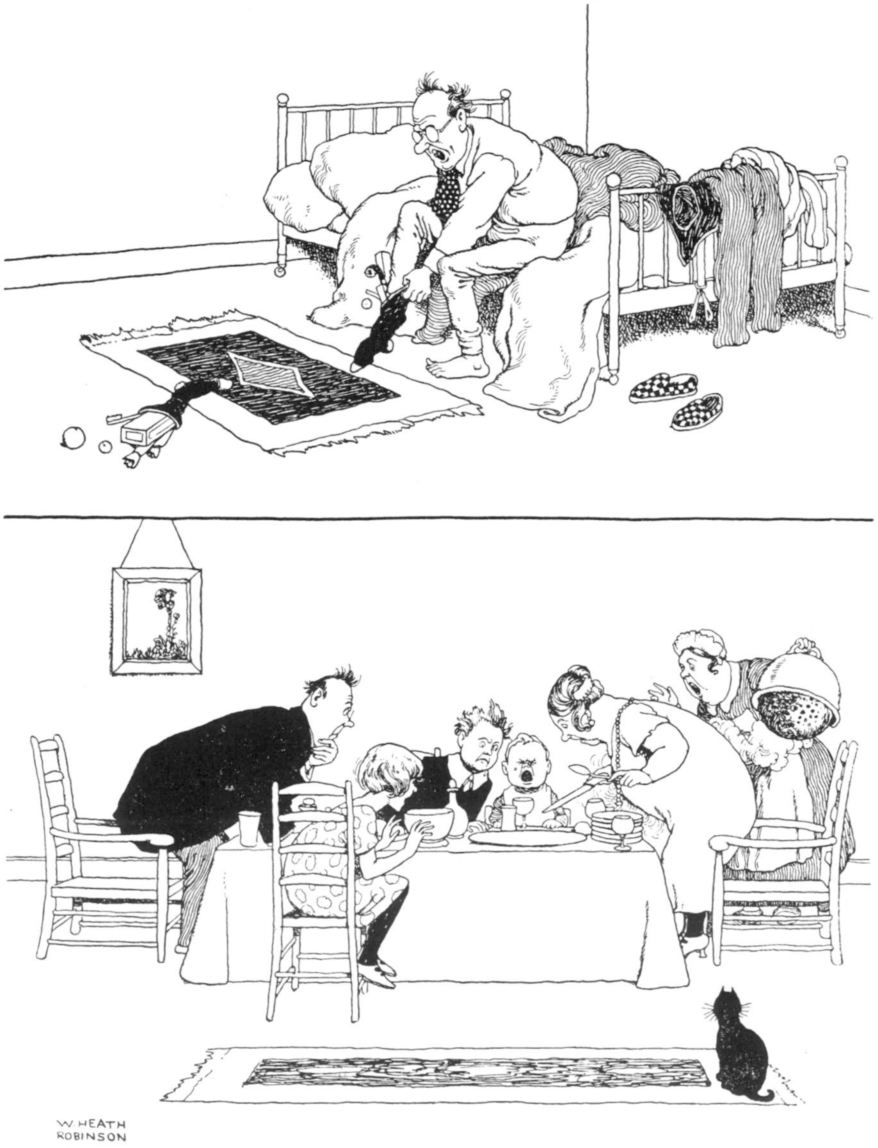
W. HEATH
ROBINSON

SPOILT CHRISTMASES

HOW TO TAKE ADVANTAGE OF THE SAVOY ORPHEAN DANCE MUSIC

THE GUILDHALL OF LONDON
On the eve of the Lord Mayor's Banquet

LAYING THE FOUNDATION STONE OF THE PROJECTED NEW STRUCTURE TO
REPLACE WATERLOO BRIDGE

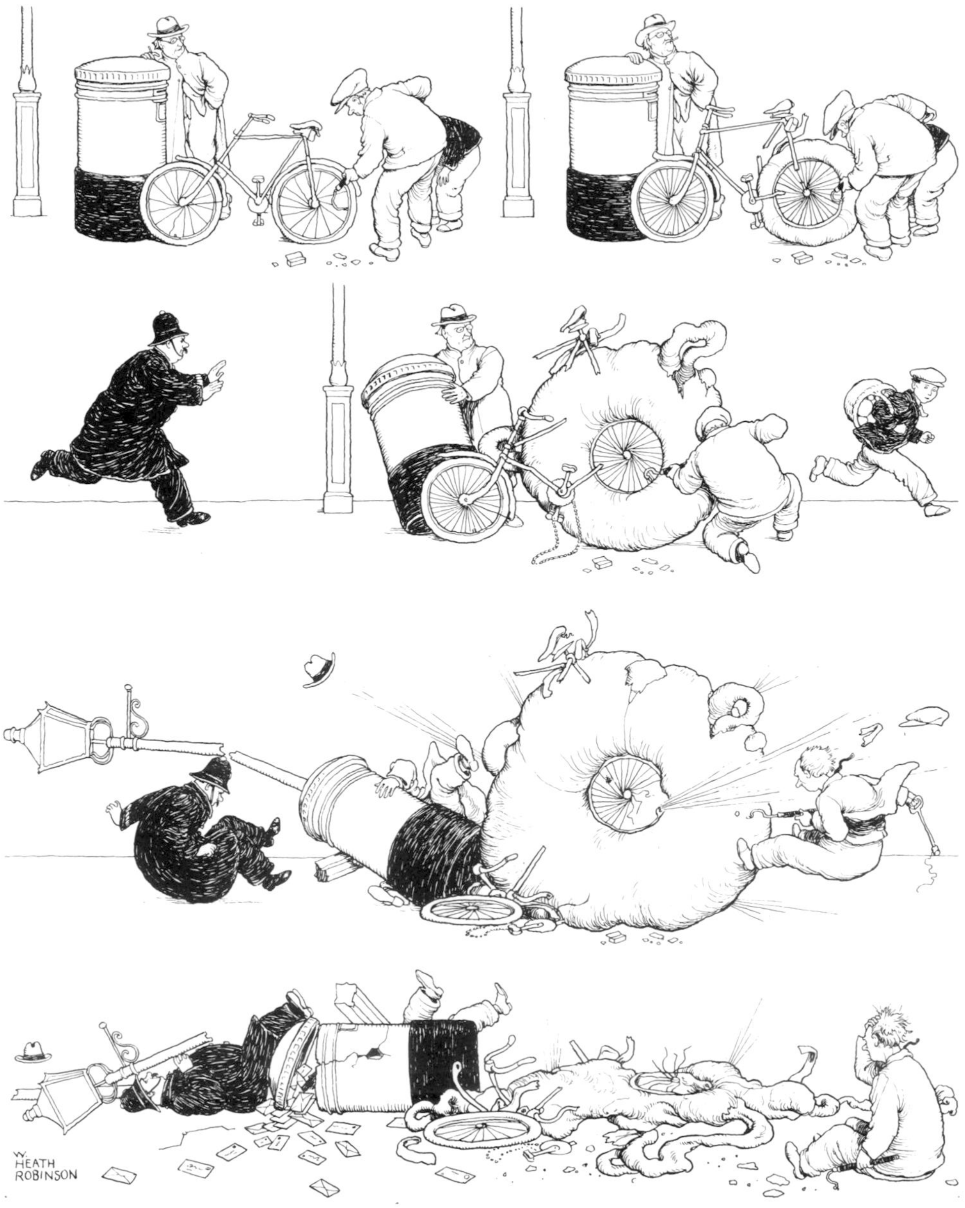
W. HEATH ROBINSON

THE PUNCTURE

THE ONLY WAY OUT OF AN AWKWARD PREDICAMENT

THE NEW MEASURING CHAIR NOW IN USE BY MOST
WEST-END TAILORS

A BUSY MORNING IN THE SUMPTUOUS STUDIO OF A FASHIONABLE HAIR ARTIST

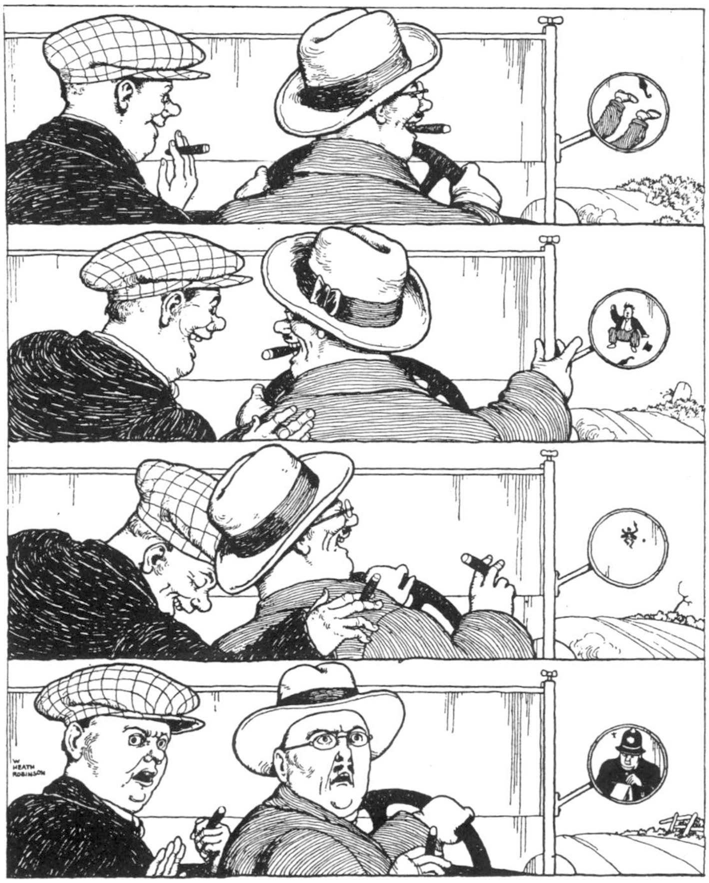
W HEATH ROBINSON

THE EYE OF THE LAW

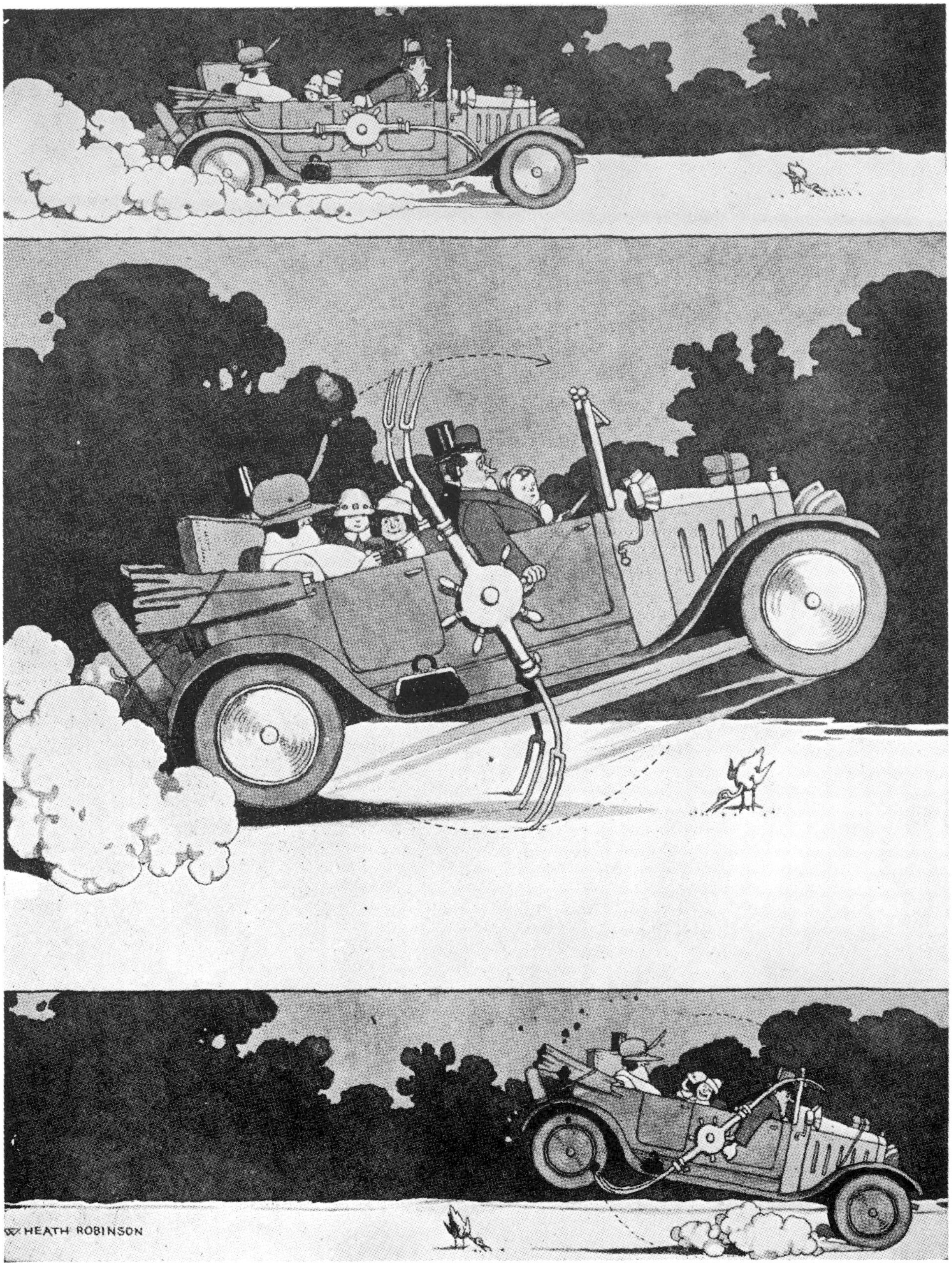
W. HEATH ROBINSON

THE NEW SAFETY-FORK ADJUSTMENT FOR MOTOR-CARS FOR THE PROTECTION OF CHICKENS ON THE ROAD

HOW THEY PUT THE TARTANS ON THE KILTS IN AN
OLD KILT-WORKS IN THE HIGHLANDS

SPRING CLEANING IN HIGHGATE WOODS

ADDING THE FINAL PING TO THE FLAVOUR
TESTING THE PIQUANCY OF A NEW BREW OF CHUTNEY SAUCE
1ST STAGE
2ND STAGE
3RD STAGE
4TH STAGE
TESTING CHUTNEY SAUCE AS A USEFUL AID TO DIGESTION
AN INTERESTING BOTTLING MACHINE ADOPTED BY ALL THE MOST UP-TO-DATE SAUCE MAKERS
AN INGENIOUS AND HANDSOME APPARATUS FOR SHAKING THE BOTTLE AND POURING OUT THE SAUCE
W. HEATH ROBINSON

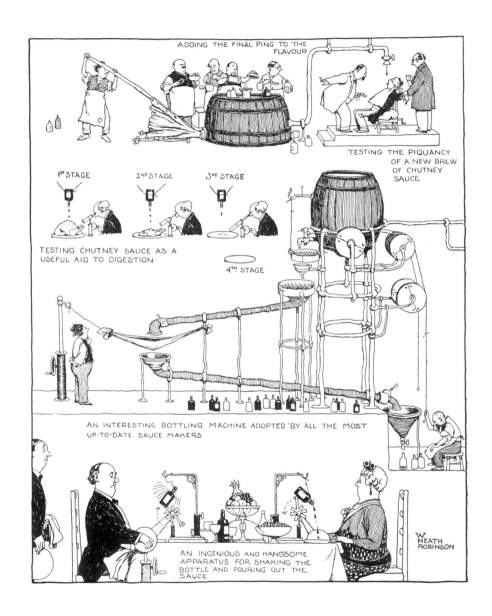

CHUTNEY SAUCE NOTES

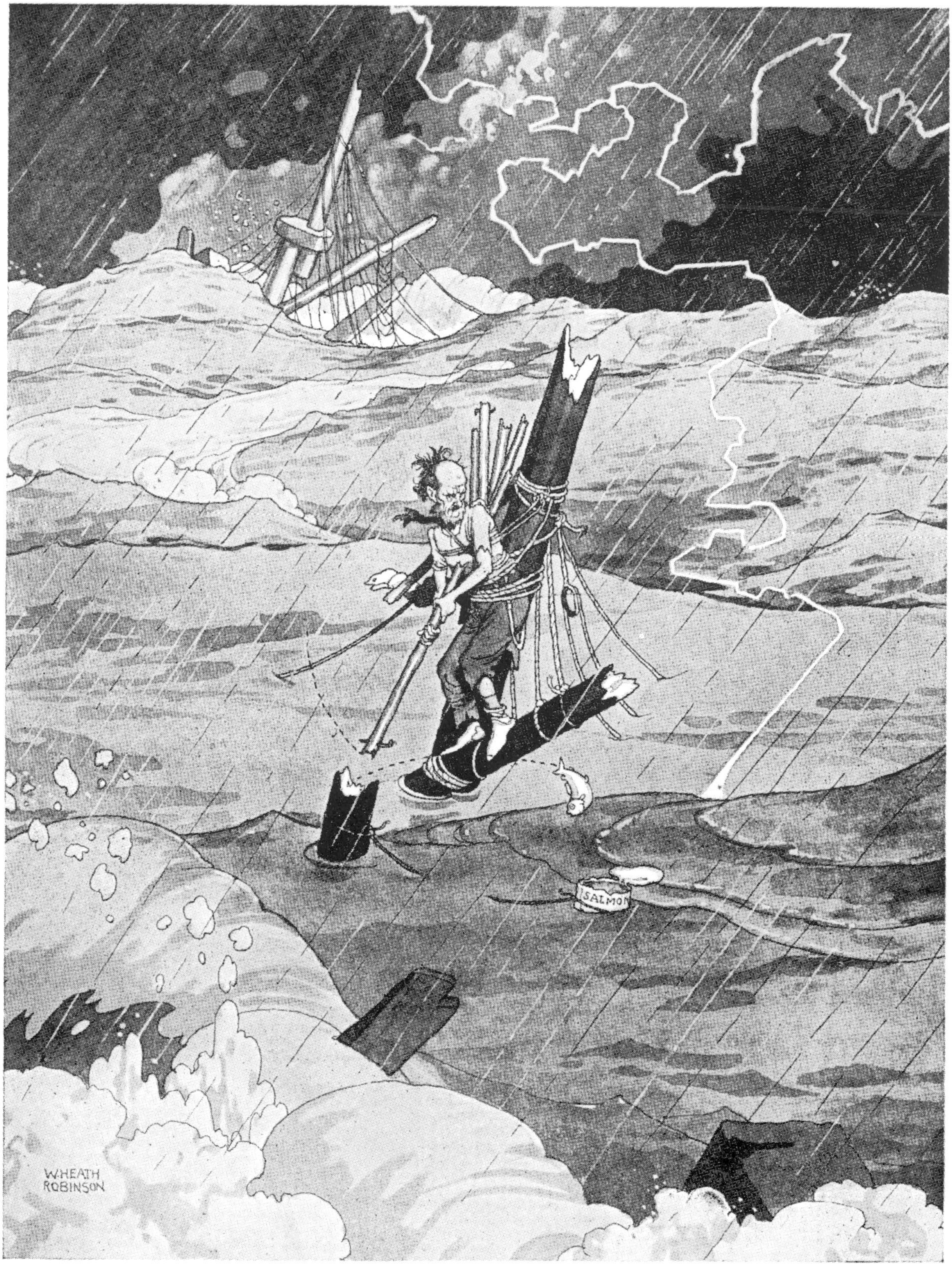
SALMON
W. HEATH
ROBINSON

INCURABLE!

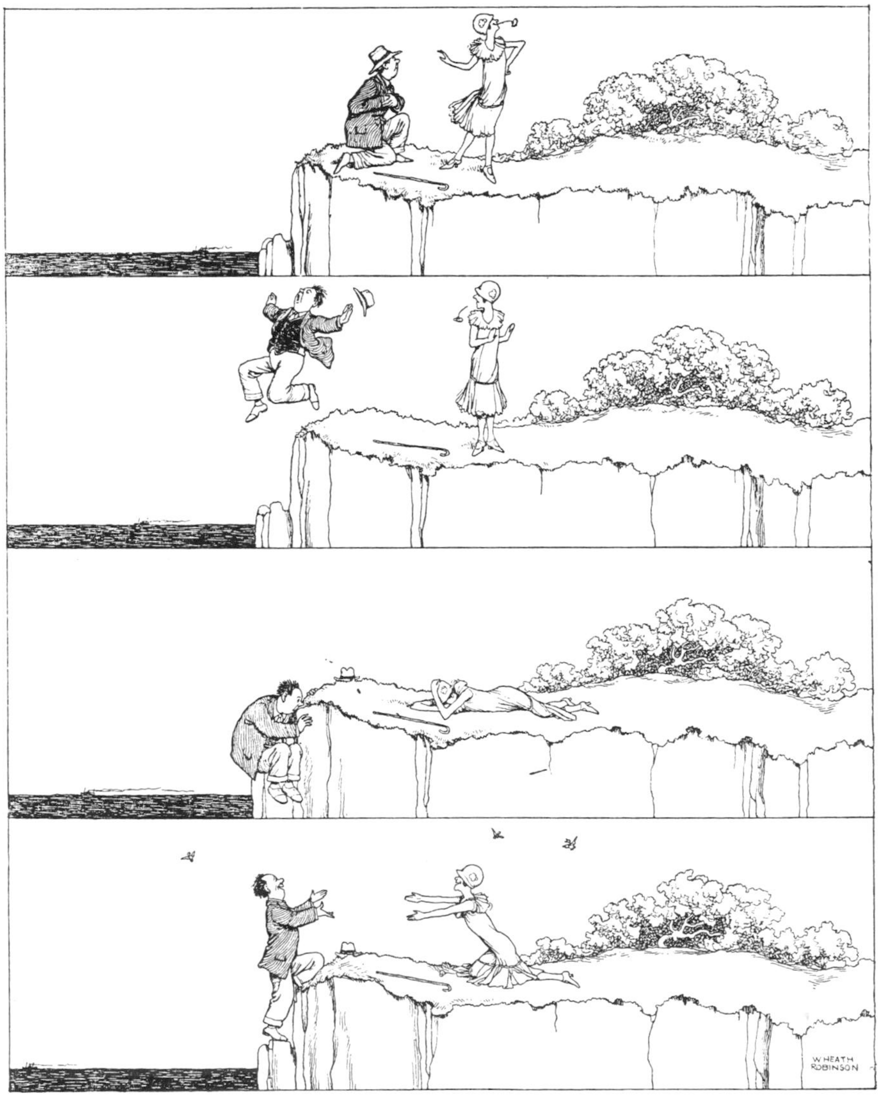
W. HEATH ROBINSON

COQUETTE

DOUBLE CROSS TENNIS

For economising space in local tournaments and generally gingering up the game

JUST A PICNIC AT WHIPSNADE

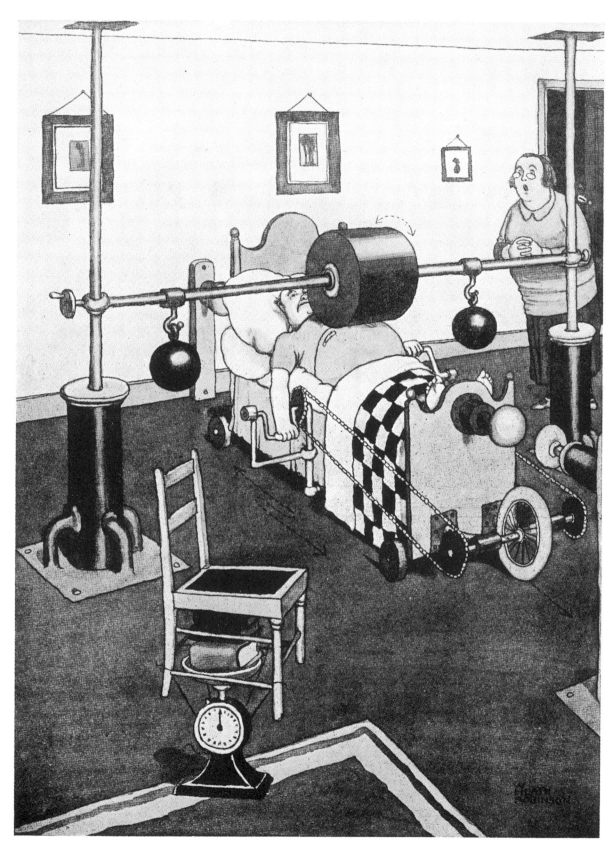

THE NEW BANTING BED FOR REDUCING THE FIGURE

HOISTING THE CHAPERONE

FLAT LIFE

Some ingenious devices for use on chilly mornings

TESTING THE WATERPROOF QUALITIES OF UMBRELLAS
IN AN UP-TO-DATE BROLLEY WORKS

FLAT LIFE

How at last it is possible to keep chickens in the top flat

35

THE WATER COUPE
An elegant little car for the convenience of anglers

FLAT LIFE
The spare bedroom

SAFETY FIRST!

New road regulations shortly to be introduced to ensure the
safety and comfort of pedestrians

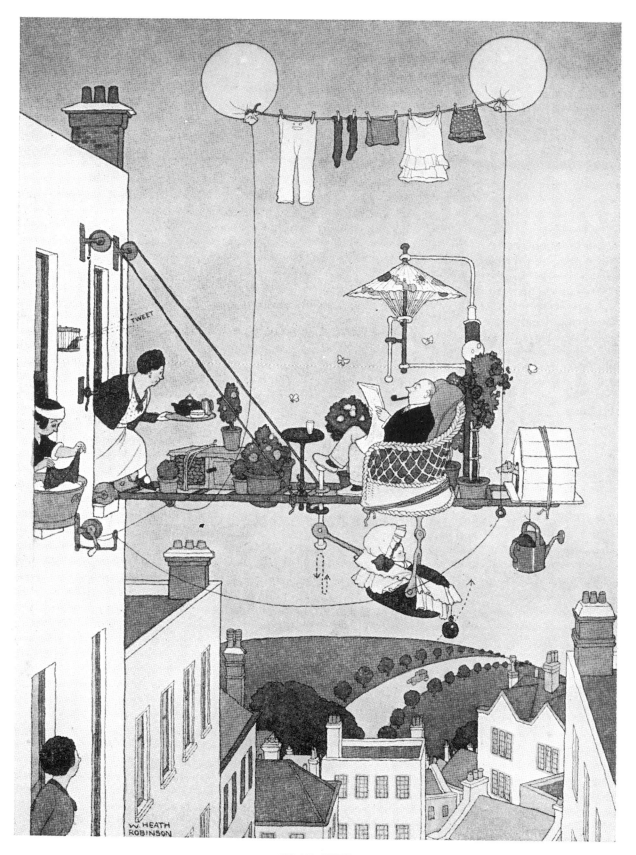

FLAT LIFE

How the tenant of the top flat can enjoy all the amenities of a back garden

FIXING UP THE NEW AERIAL

FLAT LIFE

Sane economy of space at a wedding reception

41

MAGNETIC AIDS TO SKATERS
To be installed in the London parks during the skating season

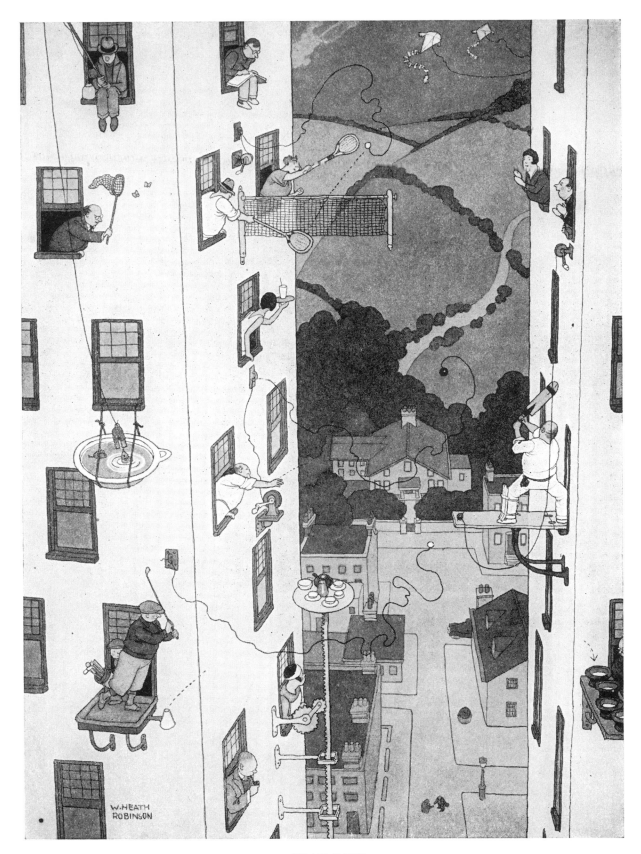

FLAT LIFE

How sport is possible on a Saturday afternoon

CHRISTMAS EVE AND THE TOY RAILWAY

SUCCESSFUL OUTCOME OF INTELLIGENT PRECAUTION OBSERVED BY OLD LADY
IN THE SOUND OF MULL

REMARKABLE PRESENCE OF MIND OF A CINEMATOGRAPHER
WHO TOOK AN INTERESTING CLOSE-UP OF HIMSELF DURING
AN ACCIDENTAL FALL FROM THE TOP OF BEACHY HEAD

INTERESTING TREATMENT OF CATTLE ON AN ARGENTINE STOCK FARM TO MAKE
THE MEAT TENDER AND SOFT BEFORE KILLING

UNDER THE MISTLETOE
Any old excuse !

TOEING FOR CRABS AT HERNE BAY

LOW CUNNING OF A COMMON PICTURE-POSTCARD THIEF

A WARM-HEARTED OLD SOUL DISGUISED AS A MERMAN SEEKING TO LURE A
MERMAID FROM HER NATIVE ELEMENT

A NOTORIOUS GANG OF HAT THIEVES AT WORK IN EPPING
FOREST ON SUNDAY AFTERNOONS

FOR THE CONVENIENCE OF BATHERS IN ROUGH WEATHER

AN AWKWARD PREDICAMENT

NEW TOP FLAT RESCUE APPARATUS

THE MULTI-MOVEMENT TABBY SILENCER
This apparatus can be operated from the bedroom window and is
guaranteed to reach any part of the back yard

HALF-HOURS AT A MATTRESS-MAKING FACTORY

EARLY MORNING AT SCOTLAND YARD
Detectives in various disguises and the Flying Squad starting out
on their morning rounds

THE STILL SMALL VOICE

Mrs. Blendlethorpe : "For goodness' sake, John, wake up at once ; there's someone calling for help in the room beneath."

THE MAN WHO COULDN'T AFFORD TO
GO TO THE ACADEMY

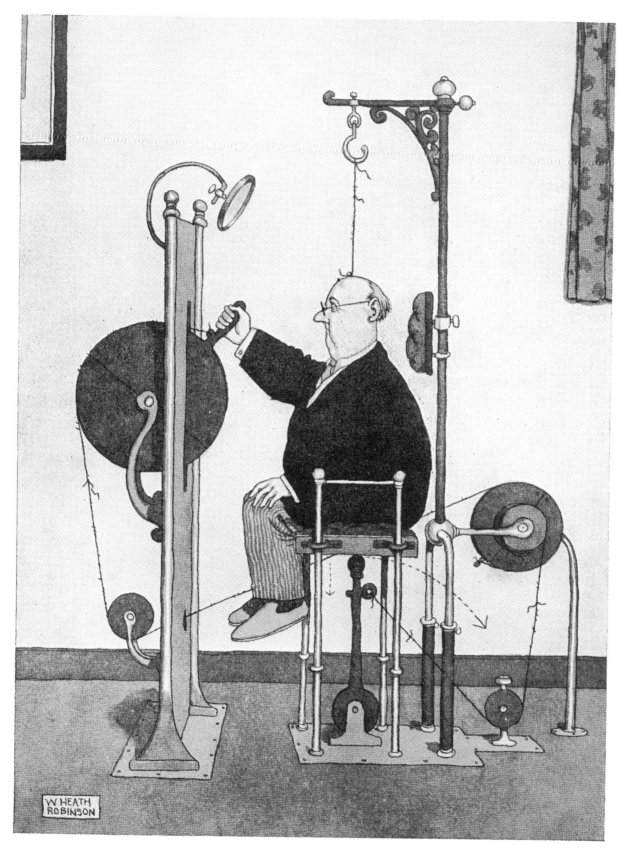

THE WART CHAIR
A simple device for removing a wart from the top of the head

LUNCHEON HOUR ON THE THAMES EMBANKMENT

HISTORY REPEATS ITSELF
An unrecorded panic at Whipsnade, owing to a spell of wet weather

SELLING IRISH SWEEPSTAKE TICKETS UNDER THE
EYES OF THE LAW

SWIMMING THE CHANNEL

Some simple devices to ensure success

SPRING AND SPRING ONIONS
An idyll of the sea

RESUSCITATING STALE RAILWAY SCONES FOR REDISTRIBUTION
AT THE STATION BUFFETS

67

THE KIND OF THING WE MUST EXPECT WHEN IT
BEGINS TO FREEZE

SQUARE PEGS INTO ROUND HOLES

THE LANGUAGE OF EGGS
Some new designs for Easter eggs to facilitate the exchange of graceful
sentiments and amorous messages

TEMPERING THE WATER TO THE SHORN LAMB
The new waterside geyser for the holidays

71

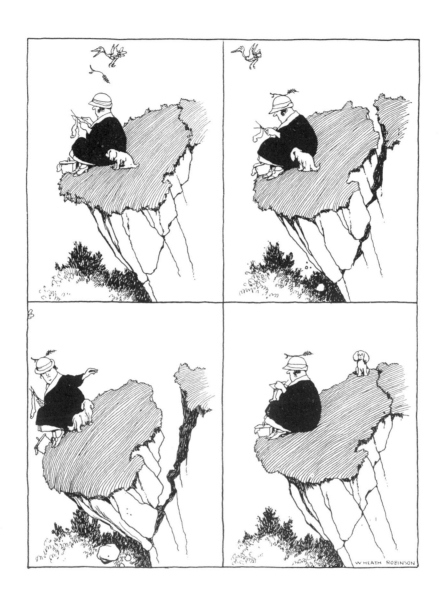

THE LAST STRAW THAT DIDN'T BREAK THE
CAMEL'S BACK

72

FISH TENNIS
A thrilling new water game

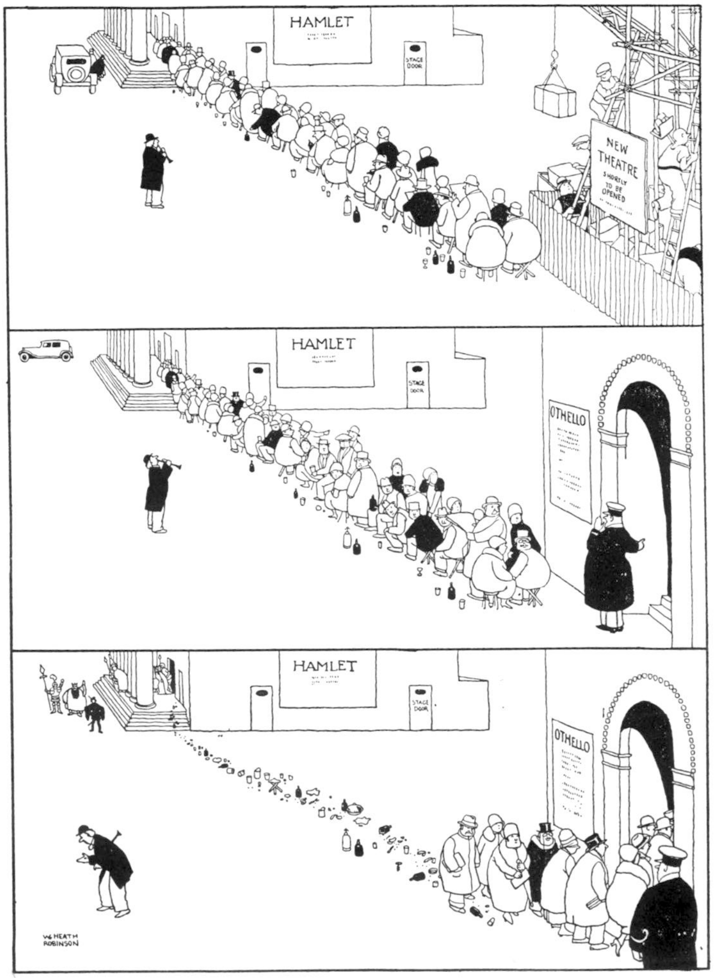
HAMLET
STAGE DOOR
NEW THEATRE SHORTLY TO BE OPENED
HAMLET
STAGE DOOR
OTHELLO
HAMLET
STAGE DOOR
OTHELLO
W. HEATH ROBINSON

THE STOLEN QUEUE

A NEW SNOW-PLOUGH FOR CLEARING A FOOTPATH AFTER A HEAVY FALL

NEW AND INGENIOUS METHODS OF ADVERTISING

A NEW METHOD OF TEACHING WOULD-BE ANGLERS TO ANGLE

ARRIVAL OF THE JUDGE, JURIES, COUNSEL AND
LITIGANTS AT THE LAW COURTS

TRAPPING THE CLOTHES MOTH IN THE WILDS OF IDAHO

MECHANICAL AIDS FOR CHRISTMAS

WHAT SHALL I PUT ON?

Bedside contrivance for the changeable season, to indicate the state of the weather and what you should wear when you get up in the morning

A NEW MACHINE ERECTED ON MARGATE SANDS FOR
DRYING THE HAIR AFTER BATHING

SOME OCCASIONS WHEN A GENTLEMAN IS NOT EXPECTED TO GIVE UP HIS
SEAT TO A LADY

SOMETHING ON EACH WAY
A Fish Tragedy

CULTIVATING BUOYANCY, TOUGHNESS AND RESISTING POWER IN HIDES FOR
FOOTBALLS IN THE STOCKYARDS OF A FOOTBALL FACTORY

THE HOME-MADE CHRISTMAS PRESENT

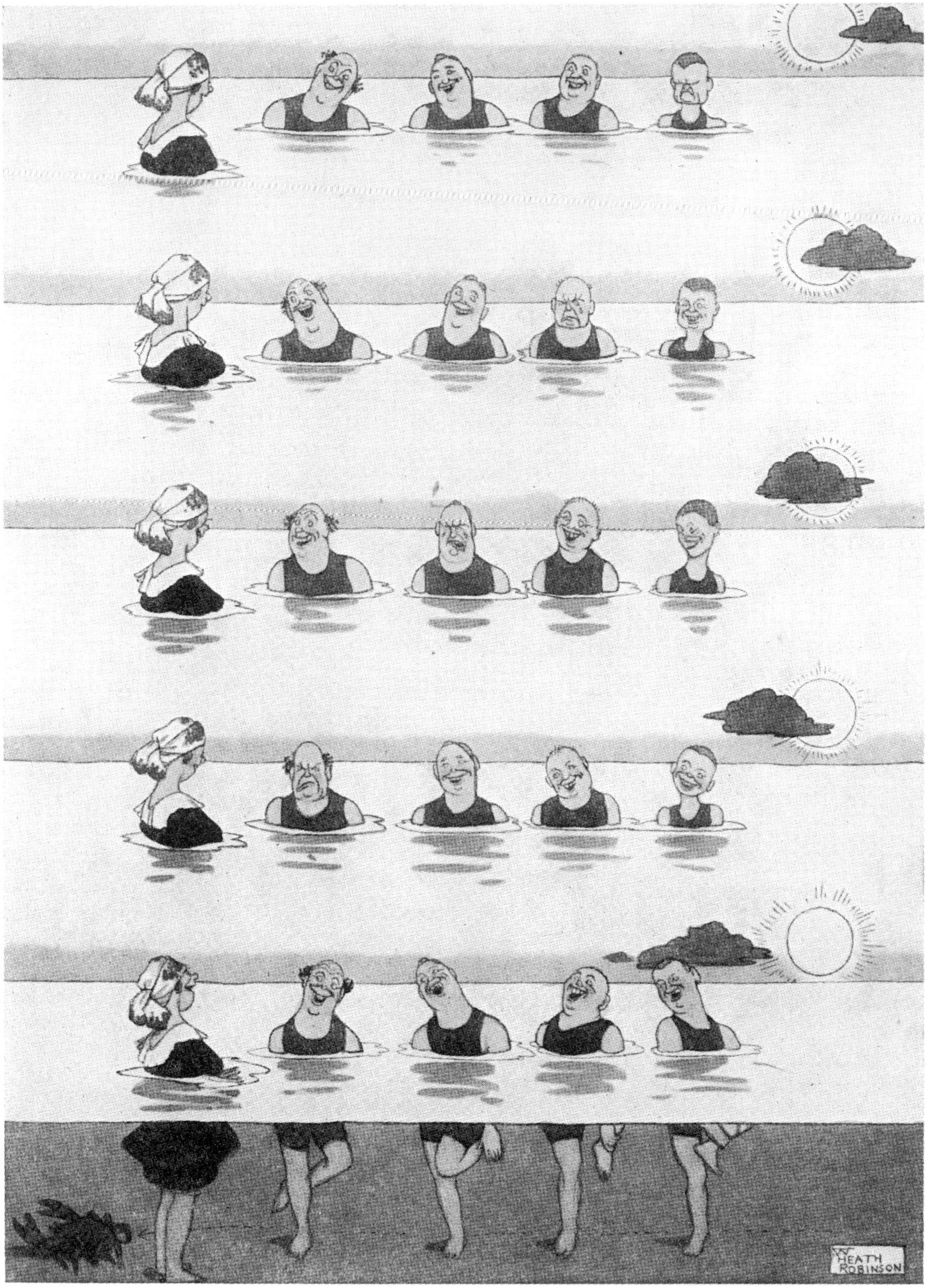
HEATH
ROBINSON

THE PASSING CLOUD

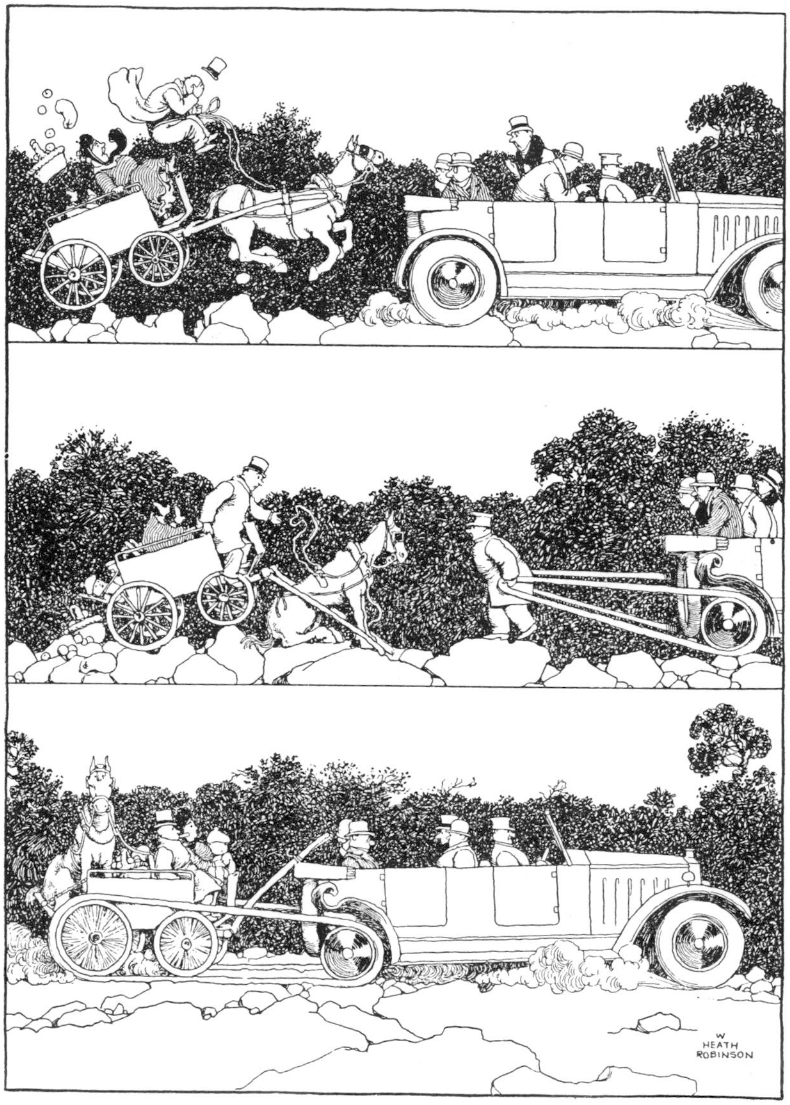
W
HEATH
ROBINSON

ELASTICITY

Disinterested conduct of kind-hearted motorists to sufferers from the bad state of the road

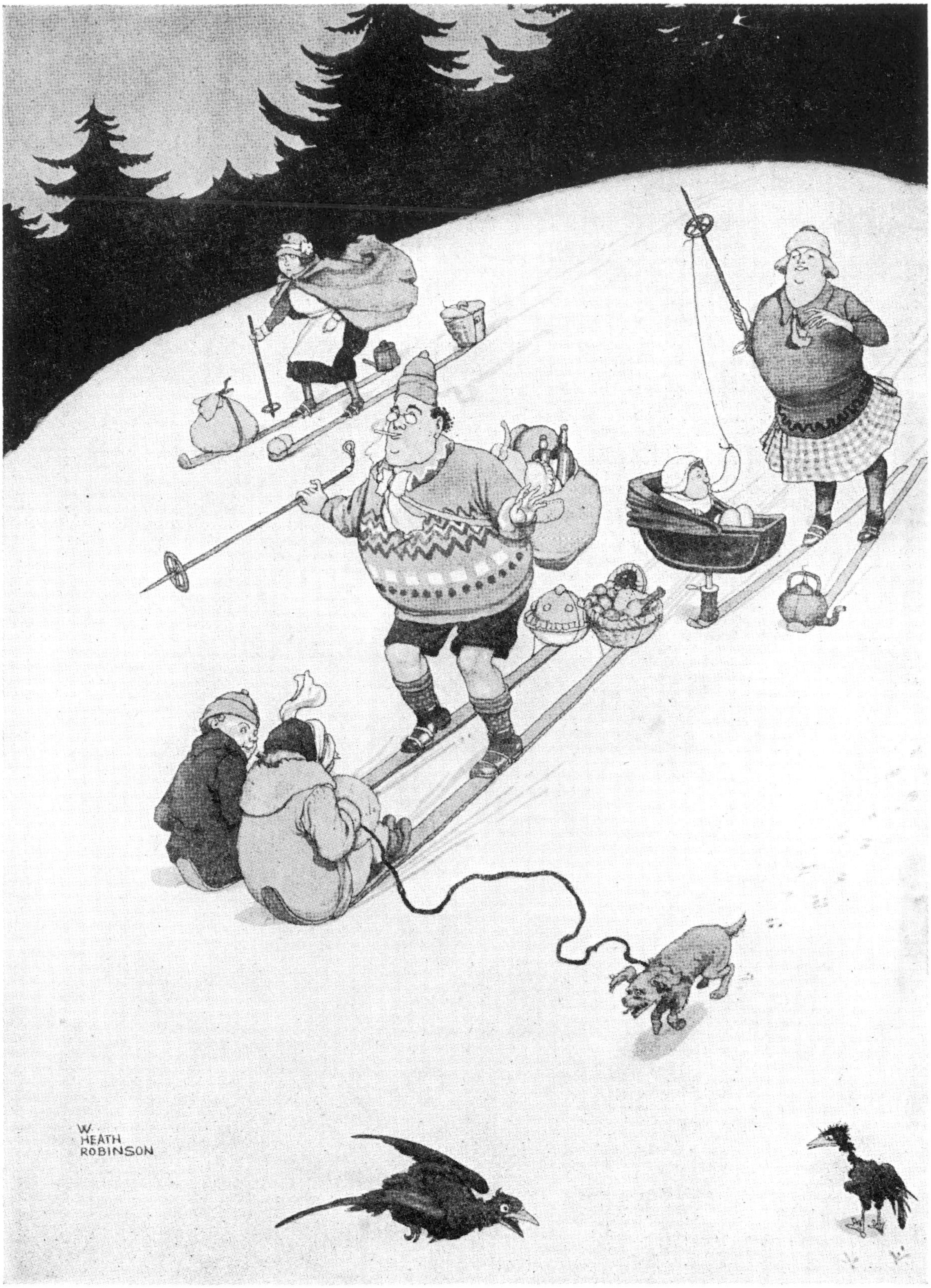
W.
HEATH
ROBINSON

OFF TO THE SKI PICNIC

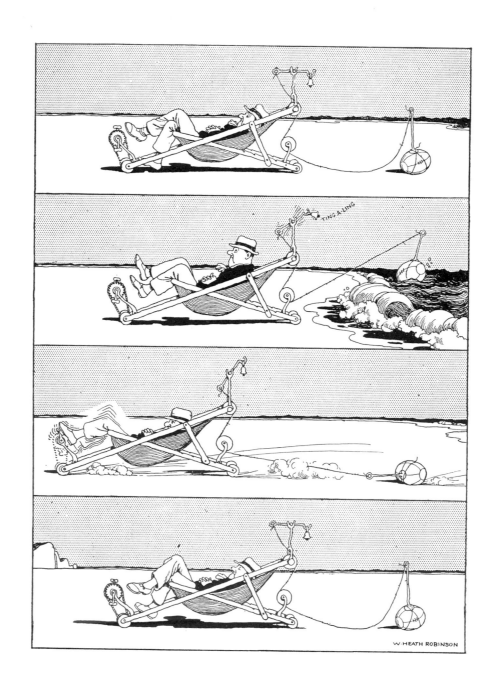

THE SAFETY DECK CHAIR FOR GIVING DUE WARNING
OF THE APPROACH OF THE TIDE

ADVERSE CRITICISM OF STATUARY

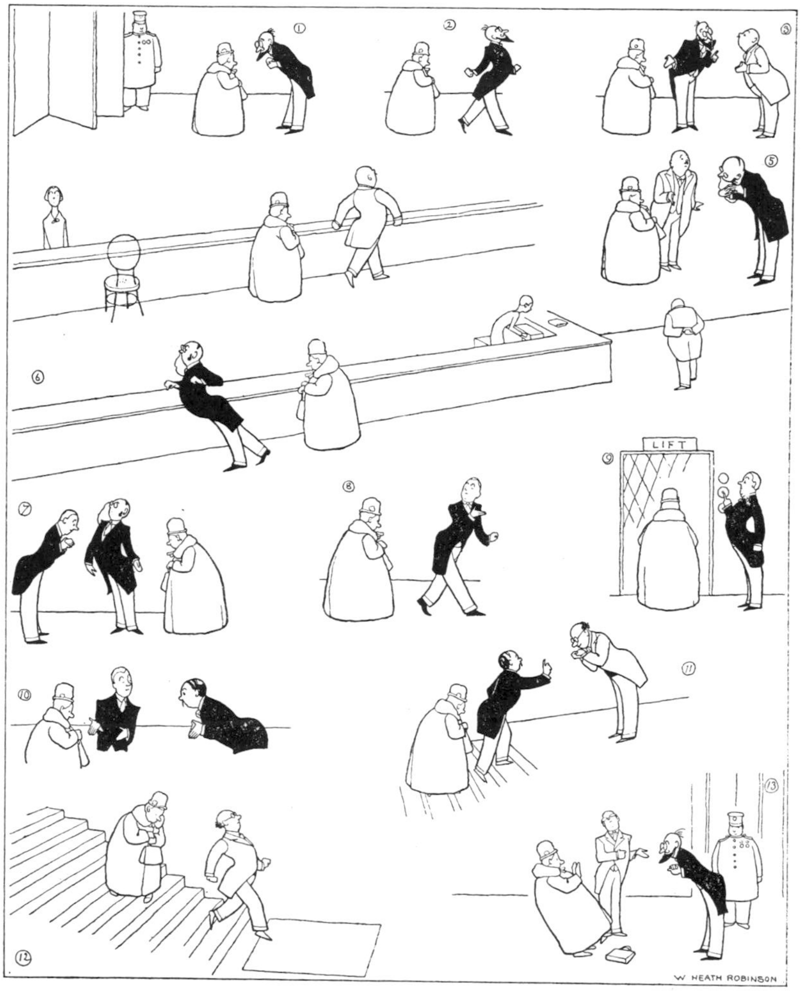
LIFT
W. HEATH ROBINSON

STEP THIS WAY

WIDGEON BLUFFING ON THE ROARING FORK

OVERCOMING THE DIFFICULTIES OF SERENADING
IN NEW YORK CITY

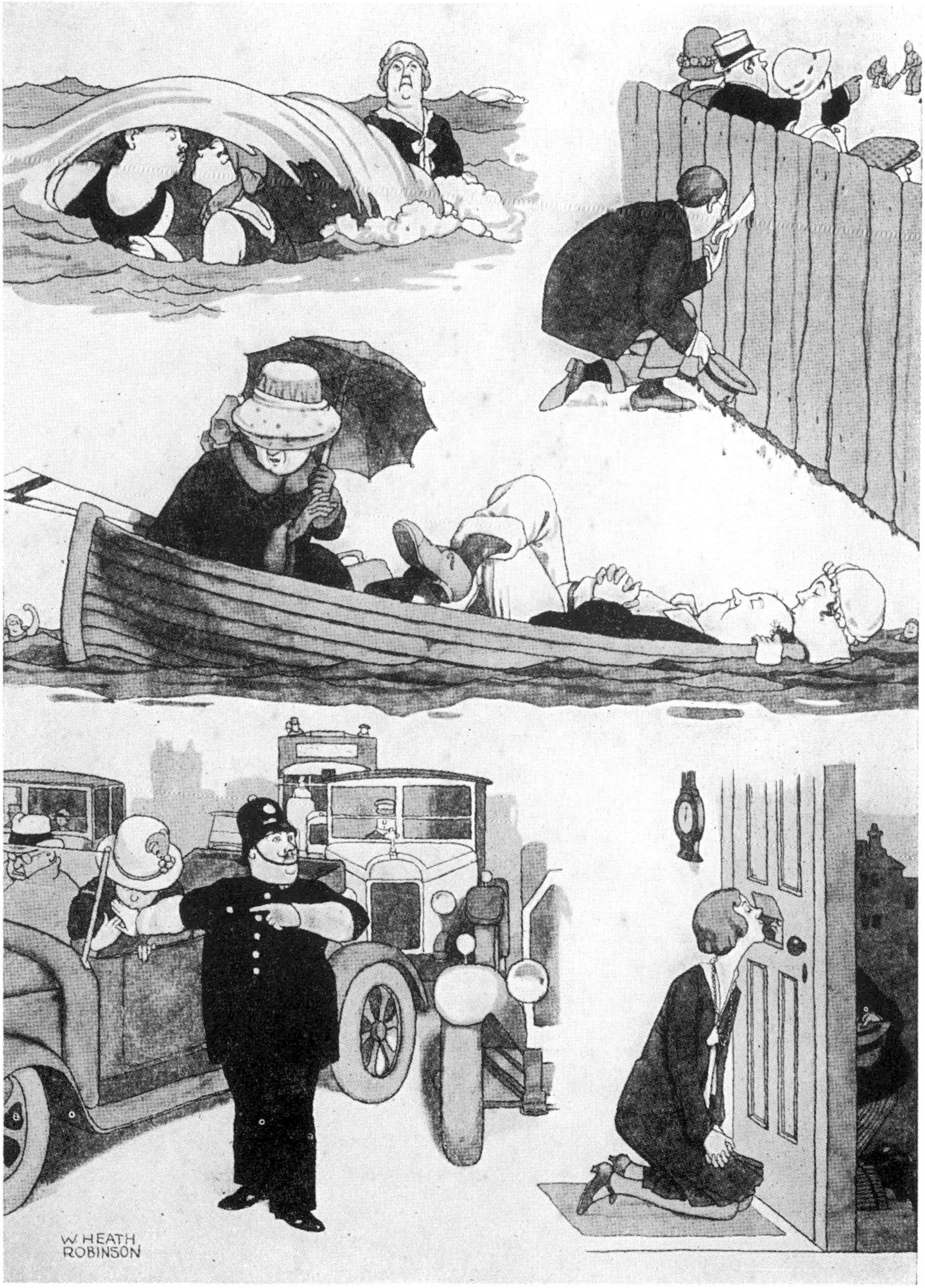
W. HEATH
ROBINSON

STOLEN KISSES

WIRELESS ENTHUSIAST
(*to sympathetic neighbour*)
"Yes, it's quite all right in theory, but somehow or
other in practice the darned thing won't work"